M257 Unit 1
UNDERGRADUATE COMPUTING

Putting Java to work

Java everywhere

Unit 1

This publication forms part of an Open University course M257 *Putting Java to work*. Details of this and other Open University courses can be obtained from the Student Registration and Enquiry Service, The Open University, PO Box 197, Milton Keynes MK7 6BJ, United Kingdom: tel. +44 (0)870 333 4340, email general-enquiries@open.ac.uk

Alternatively, you may visit the Open University website at http://www.open.ac.uk where you can learn more about the wide range of courses and packs offered at all levels by The Open University.

To purchase a selection of Open University course materials visit http://www.ouw.co.uk, or contact Open University Worldwide, Michael Young Building, Walton Hall, Milton Keynes MK7 6AA, United Kingdom for a brochure. tel. +44 (0)1908 858785; fax +44 (0)1908 858787; email ouwenq@open.ac.uk

The Open University
Walton Hall, Milton Keynes
MK7 6AA

First published 2007.

Edited, designed and typeset by The Open University.

Printed and bound in the United Kingdom by Hobbs the Printers Ltd.

ISBN 978 0 7492 0280 4

1.1

The paper used in this publication contains pulp sourced from forests independently certified to the Forest Stewardship Council® (FSC®) principles and criteria. Chain of custody certification allows the pulp from these forests to be tracked to the end use (see www.fsc-uk.org).

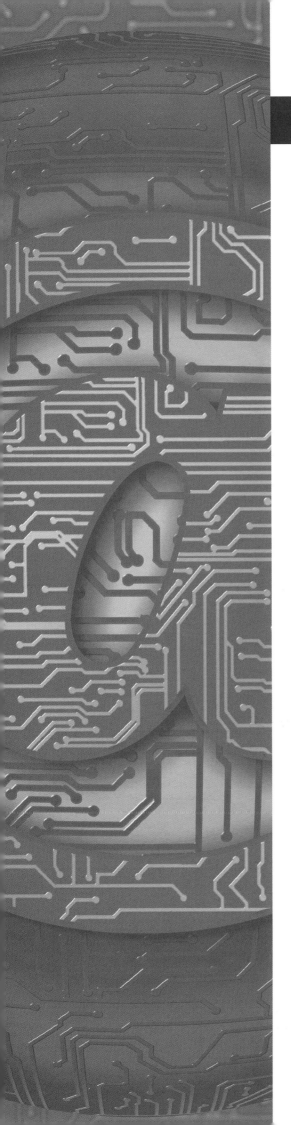

CONTENTS

1	Introduction	5
2	Java background	6
	2.1 The aims of the Java language	6
	2.2 Versions and editions of Java	6
	2.3 A simple Java program	7
	2.4 Using comments in Java programs	8
3	The system	9
	3.1 How the Java compiler works	9
	3.2 The Java Software Development Kit	10
4	Getting Java running	11
	4.1 Applications and applets	11
	4.2 Running Java applications and Java applets	11
5	Objects	12
	5.1 A simple robot world	12
	5.2 A more complex robot world	15
	5.3 Robot talk	17
6	State changes	18
7	Classes in Java	21
	7.1 Defining a Java class	21
	7.2 Naming guidelines for Java programs	22
	7.3 Creating and using objects	23
	7.4 Methods that return a value	23
	7.5 Methods that have arguments	24
	7.6 Constructors	26
	7.7 The role of the `main` method	28
	7.8 Information hiding	29
8	Inheritance	31
	8.1 The definition of inheritance	31
	8.2 Inheritance example – magic robots	32
	8.3 Overriding methods	35
	8.4 Overloading methods	37
9	Summary	41
	Index	43

M257 COURSE TEAM

M257 *Putting Java to work* was adapted from M254 *Java everywhere*.

M254 was produced by the following team.

Martin Smith, Course Team Chair and Author

Anton Dil, Author

Brendan Quinn, Author

Janet Van der Linden, Academic Editor

Barbara Poniatowska, Course Manager

Ralph Greenwell, Course Manager

Alkis Stavrinides, External Assessor, Coventry University

Critical readers

Pauline Curtis, Associate Lecturer

David Knowles, Associate Lecturer

Robin Walker, Associate Lecturer

Richard Walker, Associate Lecturer

The M257 adaptation was produced by:

Darrel Ince, Course Team Chair and Author

Richard Walker, Consultant Author and Critical Reader

Matthew Nelson, Critical Reader

Barbara Poniatowska, Course Manager

Ralph Greenwell, Course Manager

Alkis Stavrinides, External Assessor, Coventry University

Media development staff

Andrew Seddon, Media Project Manager

Ian Blackham, Editor

Anna Edgley-Smith, Editor

Jenny Brown, Freelance Editor

Andrew Whitehead, Designer and Graphic Artist

Glen Derby, Designer

Phillip Howe, Compositor

Lisa Hale, Compositor

Thanks are due to the Desktop Publishing Unit of the Faculty of Mathematics and Computing.

1 Introduction

During the early days of the **internet**, Sun Microsystems introduced the **Java** language, with great fanfare, in 1995. Java immediately generated huge interest and excitement – use of the language took off more rapidly than any computer language before or since.

Java is the language most identified with the internet and its friendly face, the web. In this course, you will learn how Java originated and how it is used nowadays. Most importantly, you will learn the language used to build systems that power so much of the web in applications ranging from e-commerce to online games, downloadable music to online banking. Java runs on servers, PCs, mobile phones and PDAs (personal digital assistants). It can be found in TV set-top boxes, in embedded devices (forming part of larger systems such as cars, robots or printers), in smart cards and even in wearable computers. Java really is everywhere.

PDAs are hand-held computers.

In this unit, we aim to:

▶ briefly outline the history of the Java programming language and the aims of its designers;

▶ highlight the wide range of platforms for which Java is available and the implications of this;

▶ show you what a simple Java program looks like and enable you to run a simple Java application, using the course software tools;

▶ explain the basic concepts of a system as a collection of interacting objects;

▶ outline the role of classes in object-orientation;

▶ show how inheritance is used to design class hierarchies.

2 Java background

In this section we look briefly at what the designers of Java tried to achieve. As with many successful inventions, it eventually went in directions that its designers had not expected. We explore how the different versions of Java are distinguished, including the concept of Java editions to cater for systems of differing scales. We also take our first look at a simple Java program.

2.1 The aims of the Java language

The developers of the Java language had a number of design goals. These were set out in their so-called 'white paper' on the Java Programming Language Environment. Later in the course we assess how successful the designers have been in meeting their aims. We list below some of the characteristics the language was to have.

▶ Simple: Java has a small, consistent core of fundamental concepts, which should make it simple to learn.

▶ Familiar: the language syntax is closely based on the popular C++ language, although reduced in complexity.

▶ Object-oriented: Java programs are structured around objects – we will explore this later in the unit.

▶ Robust: Java programs are strictly checked by software before they run and the language omits various error-prone features of C and C++.

▶ Secure: Java has special security features to ensure that programs running over networks cannot damage your computer files or introduce viruses.

▶ Portable: Java programs can easily be transferred from one platform (such as Windows on a PC) to run on another platform (such as Linux on a specialized server) with little or no change.

▶ High performance: Java programs can run fast enough for what is needed in each aspect of a program.

▶ Interpreted: we explain interpreted languages later, in Section 3, but at this stage we will just note that this is a key aspect of Java portability.

▶ Threaded: threaded languages allow a program to do several things at once, which can greatly improve performance.

▶ Dynamic: Java programs can adapt to changes in their environment even while the program is running.

2.2 Versions and editions of Java

Java has undergone some significant changes since its early versions, so it is important to have some appreciation of the way these versions are distinguished.

The first publicly available **version** of the language was Java 1.0. Although it was widely promoted as a serious language for the internet, it actually had a number of significant deficiencies. Many of these were remedied in later versions, with Java 1.2 being a standard and stable version for quite some time.

To emphasize the change, and perhaps also as a marketing tool, Sun changed the name of Java 1.2 to Java 2 version 1.2. Subsequent versions to date have followed this naming convention. At the time of writing, Java 2 is the standard language, and there have been a number of further versions (Java 2 version 1.3, Java 2 version 1.4, Java 2 version 1.5 and so on), each introducing relatively minor improvements.

In 1999, Sun recognized that the concept that one standard Java language package could apply to all sorts of platforms was not really feasible. So the concept of **Java editions** was introduced, to cater for the different needs of, say, large international business systems running on extensive networks with many servers as opposed to software running on mobile phones with very limited hardware resources. We will mostly be interested in the Java 2 Standard Edition (J2SE). Large-scale systems are catered for by the Java 2 Enterprise Edition (J2EE), which we will not consider in detail in this course. In *Unit 10* we will look at Java 2 Micro Edition (J2ME), designed for use on smaller systems with limited resources.

2.3 | A simple Java program

In order to give you a flavour of what Java looks like we have reproduced a very simple Java program below.

```
public class HelloWalrus
{
    public static void main (String [] args)
    {
        System.out.println ("The time has come");
        System.out.println ("the walrus said");
    }
}
```

This program produces screen output as follows:

```
The time has come
the walrus said
```

The first line of the program introduces a **class**, called `HelloWalrus`. When the program runs, the class gives rise to an **object**, which executes the code of the class. There are more details about classes and object-oriented programming later in this unit.

This class is defined as `public`, which means that objects of this class can be freely accessed by other objects in a larger system. The curly bracket on the line following `HelloWalrus` matches the closing bracket at the end of the example, as these enclose the whole class definition.

The code in this class is in the form of a method, in this case a method called `main`. The first line of the method is called the **method header**. We defer explaining the words `static` and `void` until later, but they are always used with `main` methods like this one. These two words are examples of Java **keywords** – words that have a special meaning in a Java program, and that cannot be used for any other purpose. The other keywords in this example are `public` and `class`.

The method header defines the name of the method (in this case, `main`) and is followed by the method body, which is enclosed in curly brackets. The `System.out.println` method displays, in a screen window, the exact text between the quotes.

Each of these two lines of code within the main method constitutes a **statement**, a single command to be carried out. Each statement is terminated by a semicolon.

2.4   Using comments in Java programs

Comments in Java can be delineated by /* and */. For example, we can add some additional information to the sample program from the previous section, to explain its purpose and to document its creation:

```
/* A simple Java program
   Author: The Course Team
   Date of creation: 01/01/01 */
public class HelloWalrus
...
```

There are two different notations to indicate that the text is a comment, and therefore to be ignored by the computer system.

Text enclosed in the symbols /* and */ is treated entirely as comment text, even if it extends over more than one line. We call this a **block comment**.

Text occurring on a line after the symbol // is treated as comment text.

If the symbol // is the first item on the line, this defines a **line comment**. These are convenient for brief comments, typically occupying one or two lines as follows:

```
// display a poetic message
```

There can also be valid code at the start of the line, followed by the symbol // and then an **in-line comment**. This is useful for a short comment applying only to the item on that particular line. For example:

```
} // end of class HelloWalrus
```

3 The system

In this section we describe the implementation of the Java language in a little more detail. In particular, we discuss the **portability** issue: that is, the way that programs written in Java can be run on many different platforms.

3.1 How the Java compiler works

In Figure 1 we show the implementation of a conventional programming language.

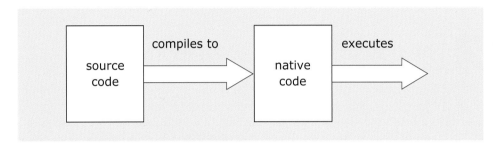

Figure 1   The action of a standard compiler

The programmer develops a program expressed in what is known as **source code**. This source code is translated by a **compiler** to the base language of the computer, known as **native code**. This is then executed and the program carries out its function.

There are strict rules governing the way source code can be written. If errors have been made, the compiler will not carry out the translation but will identify one or more compilation errors. It will issue a number of error messages to tell the programmer what has gone wrong.

This conventional way of implementing a programming language suffers from one problem – the end product is specific to just one type of computer. The native code that has been generated can be executed only by the particular type of computer that recognizes it.

In order to produce a portable implementation the developers of Java adopted the strategy shown in Figure 2.

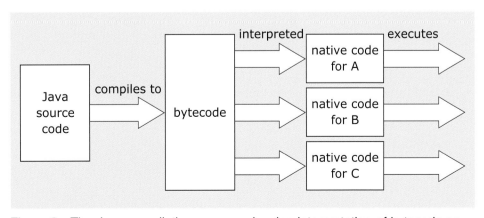

Figure 2   The Java compilation process showing interpretation of bytecode on platforms A, B and C

In the case of Java, the compiler does not translate the source code to the native code of the computer but translates it into an intermediate form, known as **bytecode**. This is a language that is capable of being executed by any computer with a suitable **interpreter**. The interpreter is a program that translates bytecode into the native code of the computer it runs on, so that it can be executed. Normally the effort in constructing a new interpreter is relatively small, and Java interpreters are available for many different platforms.

In Figure 2, the bytecode for the given Java source code is the same for the three distinct platforms A, B and C. However, there is a different interpreter for each platform A, B and C, so as to translate the bytecode into the appropriate native code for each platform.

The Java portability slogan was modified by cynics to 'write once, debug everywhere'.

This means that once a Java program has been compiled to bytecode it can, in theory, be sent to any computer that has a Java interpreter and run on that computer without any changes to the bytecode. This is the 'write once, run anywhere' philosophy promoted by Sun.

3.2 The Java Software Development Kit

The basic tools for compiling and running Java programs on a variety of platforms are freely available from Sun Microsystems. This collection of tools is known as the Java Software Development Kit, often abbreviated to the Java SDK or the JDK. This kit includes a number of important components, listed below. The names of the programs are shown in brackets but you do not need to remember these if you are using an integrated development environment, like the tool supplied with this course.

▶ The Java compiler (`javac`) translates Java source into bytecode.

▶ The Java interpreter (`java`) translates and executes Java bytecode. Java interpreters are available for many different computer systems.

▶ The document generator (`javadoc`) processes Java source files to produce useful documentation, such as standardized descriptions of what each component of Java code does.

▶ The Java debugger (`jdb`) helps developers to look for errors in programs, for example, by running only small sections of program at a time and examining the effect this has after each step.

▶ The Java disassembler (`javap`) reads bytecode files created using the Java compiler and displays the corresponding source code.

▶ The applet viewer (`appletviewer`) allows you to run and debug Java applets without a web browser. Java applets are explained in the next section.

Getting Java running

One of the main applications of the internet that has expanded well beyond the wildest hopes of its inventors has been the World Wide Web. Web documents have traditionally been written in a simple language known as **HTML** (Hyper Text Markup Language).

4.1 Applications and applets

Java programmers can produce two types of software, **applications** and **applets**. Applications are stand-alone programs, which can run independently. Applets are programs that can be included in web documents and are run using a browser. The inclusion of Java code in such documents marked a transition point in the development of the web. From being mainly a passive repository of data it became a vast array of interactive applications. Under certain conditions, users of browsers that recognize Java code can execute programs that have the functionality of programs written in any other programming language. Applets heralded a new era in dynamic content and were followed by a host of other technologies.

4.2 Running Java applications and Java applets

Before looking at the language in a little more detail, we will describe how to develop and execute Java programs. There are two main sorts of software tools that can be used.

First, you can use the Java SDK described in Section 3 (freely available from Sun), together with any text editor. In this case, the details of compiling and running a Java program may differ depending on the platform you are using for development. The various programs are normally run from a 'command line' rather than a graphical user interface (GUI) and are not seamlessly linked together.

A command line requires the user to type in the commands, rather than use a mouse and click on buttons. An example is the MS-DOS prompt on a PC.

The second approach is to use an integrated development environment (IDE), such as the tool supplied with this course. There are many IDEs available for Java, and they typically build on top of the free software from Sun, providing a sophisticated GUI and editor, with integrated facilities for compiling, running and debugging programs. Some IDEs are available for a number of different platforms. The detailed instructions for using the course IDE are supplied in a separate handbook.

In both cases, the basic development process is the same – arguably the IDE just makes things more convenient. In general, the IDE hides the details such as which compiler program is being run, or the names of the Java files at each stage.

5 Objects

In the following sections we briefly introduce the topic of object-orientation. This will serve as revision and an outline of the approach to object-orientation that this course takes.

5.1 A simple robot world

We start with a simple example, which models robots moving around a two-dimensional grid, displayed on a computer screen. The position of a robot on the grid is expressed as x- and y-coordinates, which can take any integer value within the limits of the grid. Figure 3 shows an example of a grid containing three robots. If you are not keen on robots, then you can think of this as a traffic simulation or perhaps a board game – similar principles apply.

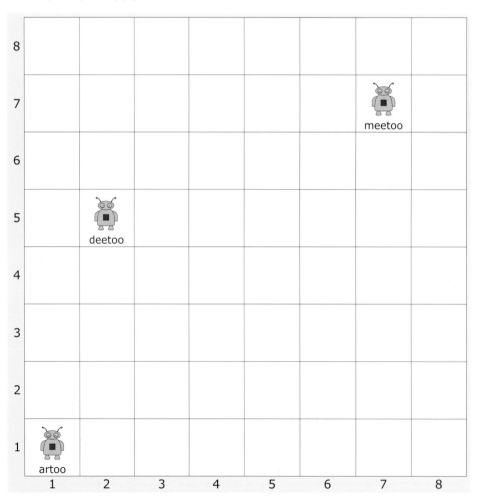

Figure 3   Grid showing the current positions of three robots

Each robot is represented by an object in the computer system. Each object has some stored data associated with it – in this case, each robot object stores its current position on the grid. The values of the data stored by an object determine the **state** of the object. For the moment, we assume that when the state of a robot object changes, the screen automatically updates and displays that robot in its new position.

We also need some way to identify each robot object, so we can manipulate the appropriate object. For simplicity at present, we assume that each robot object has a name – later on we will see that things in Java are a little more complex. So, we can think of the three robots as software objects, each with a unique name and some stored data, as shown in Figure 4.

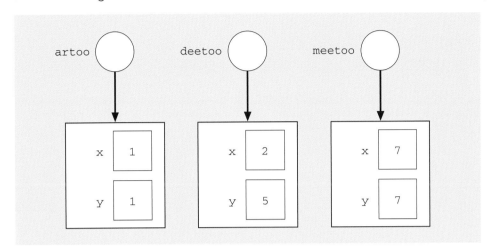

Figure 4   Software objects corresponding to three named robots

Each object can respond to a number of commands or requests. For example, a robot object may be asked to:

▶ move one position on the grid in a north, south, east or west direction;

▶ indicate its current position;

▶ move to an arbitrary position on the grid.

Objects typically have a number of operations that they can carry out on request, such as those operations listed above for robot objects. The Java code that carries out an operation is known as a **method**. Requesting the operation is known as **invoking the method** – if the method is invoked correctly, the object is then said to **execute** the method.

For example, let us invoke a method to move the robot named artoo one grid position to the north:

```
artoo.moveNorth();
```

This method invocation has two components – the name of the object, artoo, followed by the name of the method, moveNorth. The empty brackets will be explained later.

To move the robot named deetoo one position east and then one position south, we can write:

```
deetoo.moveEast();
deetoo.moveSouth();
```

To move the robot named meetoo to the position with x- and y-coordinates 5 and 3 respectively, we can write:

```
meetoo.moveTo(5,3);
```

Notice here that the brackets after the method name are no longer empty. The two numbers within the brackets are known as **arguments** – these supply information to complete the details of the request. Methods in Java can be defined to have any number of arguments. Suppose we were to omit the arguments, as follows:

```
meetoo.moveTo();
```

This would be an error – it is not clear to which position the robot should move.

Now we can see the reason for the empty brackets in the method invocations for `moveNorth` and other examples above. These are methods where no additional information is required and so these methods have no arguments. However, in such cases, the method name must be followed by empty brackets – omitting the brackets causes an error.

The effect of the method invocations above on the grid showing the three robots is shown in Figure 5.

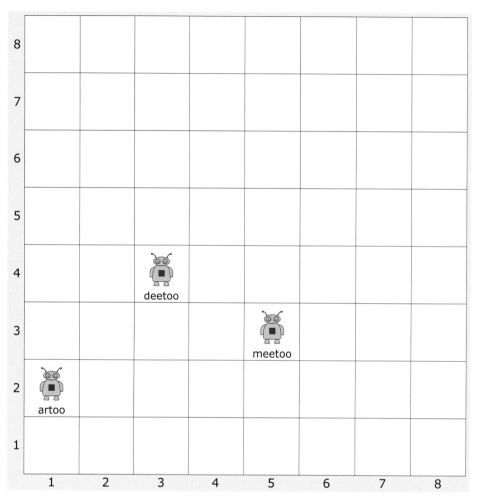

Figure 5   Grid showing the new positions of the three robots

The methods we have invoked result in the robot objects having new states, as shown in Figure 6.

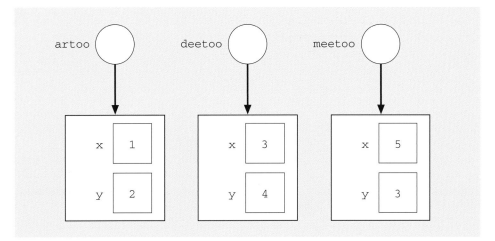

Figure 6   New states of the software objects corresponding to three robots

A software system normally consists of a number of objects, possibly many objects, which collaborate and communicate to achieve the overall aims of that system. A key idea in object-orientation is that the state of each object can normally be changed only by invoking a method.

All the methods we have seen so far can have an effect on the state of the object – such methods are known as **mutator methods** (from mutation, meaning change). Sometimes methods correspond to a simple request for information and cannot alter the state of the object. Such methods are known as **accessor methods**. For example, if we want a robot object to indicate its *x* position, we could write:

```
artoo.getX();
```

In the course M255 *Object-oriented programming with Java*, the term 'accessor method' is used to describe both methods that set and methods that get data.

This is an example of a method that produces a result. It is said to return a value – in this case, the *x*-coordinate of the robot `artoo`. This method and the corresponding method `getY` do not change the state of the object.

5.2 A more complex robot world

In the previous simple example, there was only one type of object – robots. In more realistic software systems there are many objects and a variety of different types of object. It is also possible to build up more complex compound objects, whose components are themselves objects. In this subsection, we extend the previous example to look at such compound objects.

We consider a more complex but still two-dimensional world, in which robots may be free-standing or they may travel around the grid in 'robot ships'. The robot ships are themselves named objects and they have an internal state as well as a number of methods, similar to robots. Figure 7 shows a grid containing three robot ships, each potentially containing a number of robots, together with one individual robot.

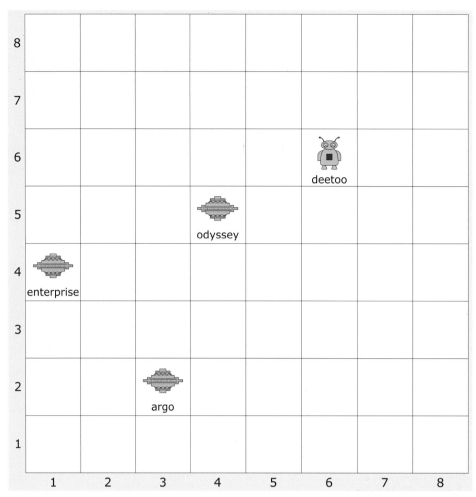

Figure 7   Grid showing position of three robot ships and an individual robot

A robot ship object can contain up to five robots. Its internal data consists of the robot objects it holds, together with a count of how many objects there are available. Viewed in terms of their internal state, the robot ships in the above grid can be represented as shown in Figure 8.

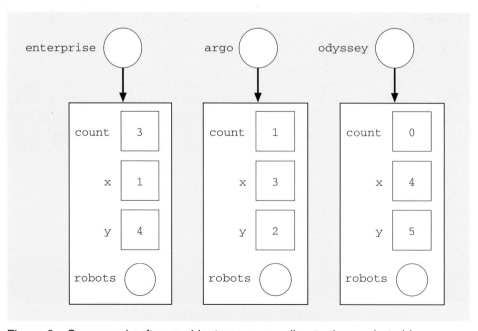

Figure 8   Compound software objects corresponding to three robot ships

All free-standing robots have an internal state indicating their position, as before. Robots enclosed in a robot ship will all have the same internal state, since they have the same position (as far as this crude grid is concerned). We will need the further assumption that a robot behaves differently depending on whether it is embarked (currently in a ship) or disembarked (not in a ship). Otherwise we could have robots emerging from ships in all directions!

We would expect a robot ship to respond to similar movement requests and position-reporting requests as for an individual robot. Additionally, a robot ship should be able to do a number of additional operations. For example, to embark a robot we could invoke a method as follows:

```
enterprise.embark(artoo);
```

The following example shows how to disembark a robot (if there are any):

```
argo.disembark();
```

In this case, the method would have to return the 'name' of the disembarked robot, so that it is available to receive requests. We shall see more detail of how this might work later in the course. The position of a newly disembarked robot is the same as that of the robot ship.

To report on the number of robots held by the robot ship `odyssey`, we could write:

```
odyssey.getCount();
```

Again this method must return a value, in this case the number of robots contained in this robot ship (which may be zero).

5.3 Robot talk

We have seen that objects have a state, represented by the values of their internal data. Compound objects have internal data consisting of one or more objects. An object can also have a number of methods, which allow other objects to access or change the state of that object. But so far, we have not seen where the method invocation comes from. Let us look at an example from the robot ship world of the previous subsection.

We have seen that a robot ship should respond to a method invocation as follows:

```
enterprise.moveTo(7, 6);
```

This should result in the robot ship `enterprise` and any robots it contains moving to position (7, 6) on the grid. Therefore the internal states of the robots within the ship should also change to ensure that they are consistent with the ship's position. But how can this be achieved? Recall that in object-oriented systems, objects cannot change the internal states of other objects directly. However, we can affect the object state by invoking an appropriate method. So when the robot ship `enterprise` moves to position (7, 6), it will need to invoke the corresponding method for any robots it contains. For example:

```
artoo.moveTo(7, 6);
meetoo.moveTo(7, 6);
```

This ensures that the robots move along with the robot ship to the new position. If the robots are subsequently disembarked from the robot ship, they will be in the correct (new) position.

6 State changes

In the previous section we told you that an object has state: the data that is contained in that object. The question that we want to address in this section is: how can we modify this data? This section aims to show this with respect to what are known as **primitive data types**.

Java has facilities for a number of primitive data types. These are values that are *simple*, for example integers, characters and floating-point numbers, as opposed to *objects*, which have a more complex structure. In this section, we are going to concentrate on integers. Since integers occupy a set amount of space somewhere in the memory of the computer and need to be identified, Java provides a **declaration** facility. An example of this is shown below:

```
int x;
int y;
int z;
```

These declarations notify the Java system that we will use three **variables** x, y and z. We can also declare several variables at once when we write:

```
int x, y, z;
```

It is normally better practice to declare each variable separately. This is easier to read and allows you to add an in-line comment describing the purpose of that variable. For example:

```
int x; // x-coordinate of robot position
int y; // y-coordinate of robot position
int z; // z-coordinate of robot position
```

These declarations cause three memory locations to be allocated. Each of these locations is uniquely identified by a label. This is shown in Figure 9. Depending on circumstances we shall explain later, these variables may have an undefined value or may have been initialized to a **default value** by the Java system (the default value for integers is zero).

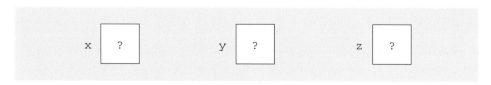

Figure 9   Primitive variables after declaration – they may or may not have a known value

The three primitive variables x, y and z usually need to be given values explicitly. This is achieved in Java by means of a statement known as an **assignment** statement, which takes the following form:

```
variable = expression;
```

where *expression* delivers some value that can be stored in *variable*. The effect of this statement is to copy the value on the right-hand side of the '=' into the variable on the left-hand side.

Initially, we consider only examples where *expression* delivers an integer result. An example of three assignment statements is shown below:

```
x = 23;
y = 333;
z = 99;
```

This results in the values being deposited in the areas of computer memory identified by x, y and z, as shown in Figure 10.

Figure 10   The effect of assignment

Assignments can be combined with declarations. For example, the statement:

```
int newPos = 99;
```

is equivalent to the code:

```
int newPos;
newPos = 99;
```

Some brief examples of more complicated expressions are shown below. In Java, + stands for addition, * for multiplication and − for subtraction. Variables on the right-hand side of an assignment are unchanged.

First, we declare and initialize some variables:

```
int oldPos = 33;
int newPos;
int increment = 3;
```

Here, we use the variables in mathematical expressions:

```
newPos = 12 + oldPos;
oldPos = (2 * increment) − 12;
oldPos = (x + y) * (x + z);
```

The first statement places 45 (33 + 12) into the location labelled newPos. The contents of oldPos are unchanged.

The second statement multiplies the contents of increment by 2, subtracts 12 from the result and then places the resultant value into the location labelled oldPos. The effect of the third statement is to add together the integers in the locations x and y, and then multiply this result by the sum of the integers in x and z, storing the final total in the location labelled oldPos.

In order to explain how this is programmed, let us examine a single Java assignment statement:

```
y = y + 1;
```

The symbol = in Java is not a mathematical statement of equality. It means 'place in the variable on the left-hand side the value of the expression on the right-hand side'. In order to explain this meaning, let us assume that the variable y contains the value 333. Then when this statement is executed, the action that is carried out is to extract the current value of the variable (333), add one to it and then place this new value (334) into the variable. This is shown in Figure 11.

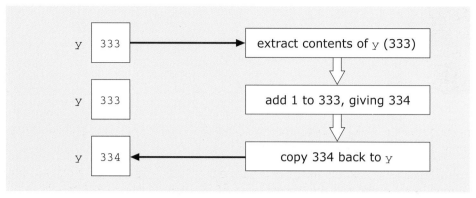

Figure 11   The effect of the statement **y = y + 1**

Some further examples of this style of assignment statement are shown below:

```
x = x + 12;
oldPos = oldPos * 2;
newPos = newPos * 3 + 1;
```

The first statement adds 12 to the value of the variable x and writes it back; the second doubles the value of the variable oldPos and writes that back; and the third trebles the value of newPos, adds one to it and places the result back in newPos.

This concludes the section on state changes. This section has been very limited in concept. All that we have tried to do is to show how primitive variables can be changed – in particular, we have concentrated on integer variables.

Activity 1.1
Executing some simple assignment statements.

7 Classes in Java

Our previous description of objects was, of necessity, brief and introductory. The aim of this section is to look at objects in more detail.

Objects in Java are defined by means of a mechanism known as a class. A class is very much like a template that defines the structure of the stored data associated with an object and the program code that is executed when particular methods are invoked. For example, all the robot objects in Section 5 could be defined as instances of a class called `Robot`. Each object of the class has the same methods and the same structure for its stored data. Only the values of the data (the state of the object) may differ between objects.

7.1 Defining a Java class

The general structure of a Java class is as follows:

```
class ClassName
{
    Data declarations
    Method definitions
}
```

The Java keyword `class` is used with an appropriate **identifier** as the name of the class. Class names conventionally start with an upper-case letter. The body of the class is delimited by curly brackets and contains both data declarations and details of the methods for the class. These items may be arranged in any order, but we will follow the convention of listing data declarations first, followed by method definitions, as shown above.

For example, the first part of the Java class definition for a robot is shown below:

```
public class Robot
{
    private int x; // x-position(W-E) of robot
    private int y; // y-position(N-S) of robot
    ...
```

This shows that the data for objects of the `Robot` class consists of two **instance variables**, x and y, which define where the robot is on the grid; these variables will hold integer values. These instance variables are declared as `private`, to ensure that this data cannot be directly accessed by objects of other classes.

The rest of the definition of the `Robot` class is made up of definitions of the methods that can be invoked on `Robot` objects. The definition of the `moveNorth` method is shown below:

```
public void moveNorth ()
{
    y = y + 1;
}
```

The first line of the definition, the method header, begins with two Java keywords, `public` and `void`. Methods are normally declared `public`, which means that they can be invoked by objects of other classes. The keyword `void` indicates that the method does not return a value. These keywords are followed by the name of the method and a list of its arguments; in this case there are no arguments, so the brackets are empty.

The method body is enclosed in curly brackets – this defines the code to be executed when the method is invoked. In this case, it consists of a single statement that increments the value of the instance variable y. This has the effect of moving the current position of the `Robot` object one grid square to the north. In the discussion that follows, we shall ignore the possibility that a robot might attempt to travel beyond the limits of the grid.

The definition of the `moveSouth` method is similar:

```
public void moveSouth ()
{
    y = y - 1;
}
```

This decrements the instance variable y by one, hence moving the robot one square to the south.

SAQ 1

Write the code for the methods `moveEast` and `moveWest`; each of these should cause the robot to move one grid square in the appropriate direction.

ANSWER..

The code for method `moveEast`:

```
public void moveEast ()
{
    x = x + 1;
}
```

The code for method `moveWest`:

```
public void moveWest ()
{
    x = x - 1;
}
```

7.2   Naming guidelines for Java programs

Note the style of names we have used for items in Java. The language is case-sensitive, so that it *does* matter whether you write a variable name in upper case, lower case or a mixture. Java keywords such as `class` or `public` must always be in lower case. You can choose the names, or identifiers, for other items such as classes and variables that you introduce.

There are standard Java conventions for identifiers, which are aimed at making programs consistent and readable – for example, a consistent naming convention helps distinguish identifiers for methods from identifiers for classes or variables.

In this course, we shall follow the standard naming convention for Java. For the parts of Java we have met so far, this is as follows.

▶ *Class names* are in mixed case, always starting with an upper-case letter, and using further upper-case letters for the start of any new word within the name. Class names will normally consist of one or more nouns.

▶ *Variable names* are in mixed case, always starting with a lower-case letter, and using upper-case letters for the start of any new word within the name.

▶ *Method names* are in mixed case, always starting with a lower-case letter, and using upper-case letters for the start of any new word within the name. Normally a method name should start with a verb.

There are similar standard naming conventions for other items, which we shall see later in the course.

7.3 Creating and using objects

Although we have not yet completed the definition of the `Robot` class, let us have a look at how the partial definition so far could be used.

In Section 6, we saw that objects have a state, methods and a name (loosely speaking). We now make the concept of an object name more precise. If we want to have a `Robot` object accessed by the identifier `artoo`, we declare a variable as follows:

```
Robot artoo;
```

This declares a variable called `artoo`, which can be used to access a `Robot` object. It is very important to realize that this declaration does not create a `Robot` object. To create an object we use the keyword `new`, for example:

```
artoo = new Robot();
```

This statement allocates memory space for the data stored by a `Robot` object. The variable `artoo` is said to reference the `Robot` object.

It is possible to combine the two previous statements into one statement that declares a variable, creates an object and sets the variable to reference the object, as follows:

```
Robot artoo = new Robot();
```

To declare variables and create objects for three robots, as in the example of Section 5, we would need the following code:

```
Robot artoo;
Robot deetoo;
Robot meetoo;

artoo = new Robot();
deetoo = new Robot();
meetoo = new Robot();
```

Following these statements, we can now invoke methods on the newly created objects, using the syntax we have seen earlier. For example:

```
artoo.moveNorth();
meetoo.moveEast();
```

Executing these methods will cause the `Robot` objects referenced by `artoo` and `meetoo` to move one grid square to the north and one grid square to the east respectively.

7.4 Methods that return a value

As well as methods that move the robot, we also have methods that indicate the current position of the robot. The two methods we need are called `getX` and `getY`. These methods each *return* a value, the current `x` or `y` position of the `Robot` object.

The code for these two methods is shown below:

```java
public int getX()
{
    return x;
}

public int getY()
{
    return y;
}
```

The method header includes the keyword `int` (rather than `void` as before) to indicate that the method will return an integer value. In the body of the method, the `return` keyword precedes the value to be returned. In this case, the methods simply return the value of the appropriate instance variable.

In previous discussions of methods that return a value, we have not explained what happens to the returned value after the method has done its work. By way of explanation, we now look at the method `getX`. We can invoke this method to find the current x position of the `Robot` object referenced by `deetoo` as follows:

```java
deetoo.getX();
```

However, this statement is not very useful as we have not made use of the returned value – in this case, it would be discarded. The simplest thing to do is to save the value by assigning it to an integer variable as follows:

```java
int currentX;
currentX = deetoo.getX();
```

We can then use this saved value in any way appropriate to an integer value. For example, we could display it in a message:

```java
System.out.println("Robot at x = " + currentX);
```

7.5   Methods that have arguments

Most methods we have described so far have had no arguments. Invoking the `moveTo` method causes a robot to move from its current position to a new point, specified by two arguments as follows:

```java
meetoo.moveTo(5, 1);
```

The code to be executed in response to such a method invocation is defined within the `Robot` class. The code required for this method is shown below:

```java
public void moveTo (int nextXPos, int nextYPos)
{
    x = nextXPos;
    y = nextYPos;
}
```

The method header shows that this method returns no value and has two integer arguments, `nextXPos` and `nextYPos`. The two arguments specify the desired next position of the robot.

The arguments `nextXPos` and `nextYPos` are known as **formal arguments**. The values used as arguments when the method is invoked (such as 5 and 1 in the above example) are known as **actual arguments**.

To put it another way – when the method is invoked, every occurrence of a formal argument in the method body is replaced by the value of the corresponding actual argument. So if we have the following method invocation:

```
meetoo.moveTo(3, 2);
```

then the code of the method `moveTo` will be executed as follows:

```
replace formal argument nextXPos by actual argument 3;
replace formal argument nextYPos by actual argument 2;
```

Here is the original code for the method body:

```
x = nextXPos;
y = nextYPos;
```

Making the replacements results in the following statements to be executed:

```
x = 3;
y = 2;
```

This updates the instance variables `x` and `y`, and hence the state of the `Robot` object.

The name of a method together with the number and types of its arguments is known as the method **signature**. This defines what is needed in order to invoke the method.

SAQ 2

What is the signature of each of the following methods?

(a) `moveTo`

(b) `moveNorth`

(c) `getX`

ANSWERS ....

(a) `moveTo(int, int)`

This shows that the method has two arguments, both of which are of type `int`. Note that only the number and type of the arguments need be shown – the formal argument name is not necessary. So far, we have seen only arguments of type `int`, but many other types are possible.

(b) `moveNorth()`

The empty brackets make it clear that no arguments are required.

(c) `getX()`

Again, no arguments are required. Although this method returns a value, this information is not part of the signature.

7.6 Constructors

We have seen earlier that objects are created using the `new` operator, for example:

```
Robot meetoo = new Robot();
```

This allocates memory space for a `Robot` object that is referenced by the variable `meetoo`. Given what we have done so far, this particular form of object creation would initialize the instance variables of the object with default values. The default value for variables of type `int` is zero, so this would create a robot initially at position (0, 0).

Java allows us to give an object a specific initial state when it is created. To do this, you must declare a **constructor** within the class.

For example, in our `Robot` class we would need to define the constructor as follows:

```
public Robot ()
{
    x = 1;
    y = 1;
}
```

The effect of this is that whenever you create a `Robot` object, for example in:

```
Robot artoo;
artoo = new Robot();
```

the resulting robot will be positioned at `(1, 1)`. The occurrence of the class name `Robot` following the `new` operator is actually a way of invoking the constructor.

Like methods, constructors can have arguments – these allow initial values to be specified for the object when the constructor is invoked, rather than having fixed initial values coded into the body of the constructor.

For example, a `Robot` constructor that sets the initial x position and y position of a robot is shown below:

```
public Robot (int xPos, int yPos)
{
    x = xPos;
    y = yPos;
}
```

We could invoke the constructor as follows:

```
Robot deetoo;
deetoo = new Robot(6, 5);
```

To summarize, we set out the complete code for the Robot class; notice that two constructors are used:

```java
// models an on-screen robot on a 2-D grid
public class Robot
{
    // instance variables
    private int x; // x-position(W-E) of robot
    private int y; // y-position(N-S) of robot

    // constructors
    public Robot ()
    {
        x = 1;
        y = 1;
    }

    public Robot (int xPos, int yPos)
    {
        x = xPos;
        y = yPos;
    }

    // methods
    public void moveNorth ()
    {
        y = y + 1;
    }

    public void moveSouth ()
    {
        y = y - 1;
    }

    public void moveEast ()
    {
        x = x + 1;
    }

    public void moveWest ()
    {
        x = x - 1;
    }

    public void setX (int xPos)
    {
        x = xPos;
    }

    public void setY (int yPos)
    {
        y = yPos;
    }

    public int getX ()
    {
        return x;
    }
```

```
        public int getY ()
        {
            return y;
        }

        public void moveTo (int xPos, int yPos)
        {
            x = xPos;
            y = yPos;
        }
    } // end of class
```

SAQ 3

(a) What are the standard Java naming conventions that apply to variables, classes and methods?

(b) What is the standard way to format these names?

   (i)   A variable called `thelastrobot`.

   (ii)   A class called `flyingrobot`.

   (iii) A method called `movetherobotforward`.

ANSWERS ....

(a) All of them use mixed-case naming where the separate words making up a name are written together, without any spaces and in lower case except for the first letter of each word being in upper case. For variables and for methods, the first letter of the whole name should also be in lower case. For classes the first letter of the whole name should be in upper case.

There are some additional grammatical conventions in addition to the conventions on upper and lower case in names. For example, method names normally start with a verb.

None of the Java naming conventions are enforced by the compiler. You can call items almost anything you like, but note that the compiler is case-sensitive; for example, `userID` is different from `UserId`.

(b) The convention for these names is:

   (i)   `theLastRobot`

   (ii)   `FlyingRobot`

   (iii) `moveTheRobotForward`

7.7   The role of the `main` method

All Java code is structured into classes and these give rise to objects when a program is run. So the methods of an object must be invoked by some code in another object (or even a method in the same object). This just leads to the further question of how this object gets created, and so on, indefinitely. Clearly, there must be a starting point for the whole business of creating objects and invoking their methods. In Java, this is the role of the `main` method. Let us now see how we can use a `main` method to test the `Robot` class.

First, we need to define a class that can be used to carry out the testing – let us call it TestRobot. This class will have a main method, defined in the way we saw earlier, as follows:

```
public class TestRobot
{
    public static void main (String [] args)
    {
        ...
```

All main methods are declared in this way.

When we run a compiled program made up of the classes Robot and TestRobot, the Java system starts at the main method and follows the Java instructions there. In this case we need to test some robots, so we must create one or more robots and then invoke their methods:

```
public class TestRobot
{
    public static void main (String [] args)
    {
        // declare variables to reference Robots
        Robot artoo;
        Robot deetoo;

        // create two Robot objects
        artoo = new Robot ();        // default starting position (1, 1)
        deetoo = new Robot (2, 5);            // initially at x = 2, y = 5

        // move the Robot named artoo one position East
        artoo.moveEast ();

        // move the Robot named deetoo
        // one position West and then one position North
        deetoo.moveWest ();
        deetoo.moveNorth ();
    }
}
```

It would actually be possible to put this main method into the class Robot, rather than creating a new TestRobot class. However, this is not normally good practice. It is better for the Robot class to be more general purpose, so it could potentially be used in lots of different programs. Keeping the main method separate makes the Robot class more flexible.

Activity 1.2
Developing a simple
Robot class.

7.8 Information hiding

This approach of defining classes and objects to control access to data may seem rather elaborate. Why would we want to do things this way?

Later in this unit you will see how inheritance, one of the more advanced facilities related to classes, can facilitate code reuse – that is, you can extend and adapt classes written for one purpose to reduce the effort involved in producing a different software system.

Apart from reuse there is also the advantage of maintainability.

Software systems are subject to major changes in their lifetime. Surveys have suggested that as much as 80% of the development effort expended by many software companies is devoted to modifying existing systems.

When you define objects using classes you can restrict access to the instance variables of an object: normally all access to the information stored in an object is via methods. This principle is known as **information hiding**: the code using an object cannot access or make use of the details of how that object is implemented.

This means that when a developer wants to change the implementation of an object (for example, to improve its performance or security) then the instance variables and program code of the methods may change but the external interface to the object – the method names and arguments themselves – does not change. So, there is no need to change any other parts of the software system that invoke the methods of this revised object, as long as the external interface has not changed.

8 Inheritance

So far we have outlined how to construct objects in Java and how to define their methods. We have also seen how classes are a sort of template to define the data structures and methods of similar objects. This section introduces another important concept in Java – **inheritance**.

In order to introduce the idea, we will look at some simple extensions to the robot world discussed earlier. Later units of the course show how inheritance is used in more complex applications.

8.1 The definition of inheritance

Inheritance is a relationship between classes. We have seen the example of the Robot class – all objects of this class have exactly the same structure for their data (their instance variables) and exactly the same methods that can be invoked.

In more complex systems, we often identify a need for various objects that are similar in structure, but not exactly the same. Inheritance gives us a way of documenting this similarity and of using it in the Java implementation. We will start with a broad definition, which we will make more precise in a later unit.

When a class B inherits from a class A, then objects of class B are in some sense extended versions of class A objects. They have all the same methods and instance variables as class A objects; they can also have additional methods and instance variables, or can modify the methods they inherit, so that a class B object typically behaves in some ways like a class A object, but in other ways behaves differently.

When a class B inherits methods and variables from a class A, then B is known as the **subclass** of A and A is known as the **superclass** of B. There is a standard graphical notation for this, as shown in Figure 12 – the arrow always points from the subclass to the superclass. The diagrammatic notation used here is part of the Unified Modeling Language (or UML for short).

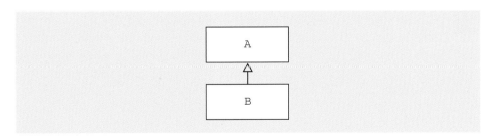

Figure 12   UML diagram of class B inheriting from class A

In Java, a class can inherit directly from only one other class: that is, it can have only one immediate superclass. This is not true of all object-oriented languages, but it is a deliberate choice by the Java language designers to avoid some well-known problems that might otherwise arise. On the other hand, a class can have more than one subclass, as shown in Figure 13. In fact, it can have any number of subclasses.

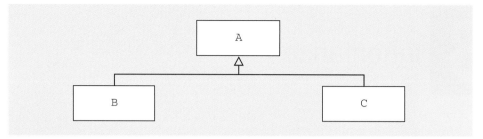

Figure 13   UML diagram of classes B and C inheriting from class A

It is also possible to have more levels of inheritance, as shown in Figure 14. Subclass B may itself have a subclass, class D. Objects of class D are extended versions of class B objects. They have all the same methods and instance variables as class B objects, including those that B inherited from class A. They can also have additional methods and instance variables, or can modify the methods they inherit.

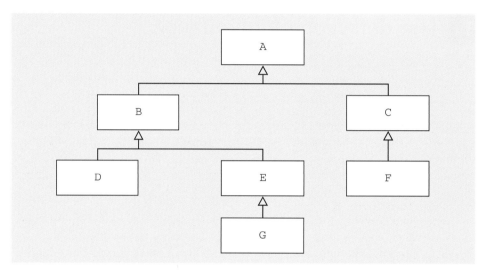

Figure 14   UML diagram showing several levels of class inheritance

This form of diagram, which shows the inheritance relationships between classes, is known as a **class hierarchy** diagram. Class hierarchies are a very powerful way of describing the relationship between classes. This relationship lies at the heart of the use of an object-oriented programming language as a medium for software reuse.

8.2 Inheritance example – magic robots

As an example of inheritance, let us consider broadening the world of robots to admit a different sort of `Robot` with additional special abilities. We can define a `MagicRobot` that is able to move around in the same way as an ordinary robot, but is also able to become invisible, so that it does not show up on the screen display. This property could clearly be useful if we are using the robots as part of a game. Perhaps less obviously, it could be used in a practical robotics application, to reduce clutter by allowing selective display on a grid containing many robots.

In Java we say that the subclass extends its superclass – for example, the start of the `MagicRobot` class definition looks like this:

```
public class MagicRobot extends Robot
{
    ...
```

This is shown diagrammatically in Figure 15, using UML notation.

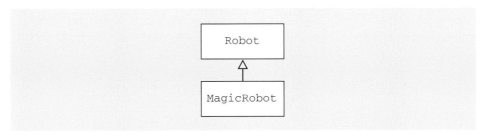

Figure 15   UML diagram showing **MagicRobot** inheriting from **Robot**

Since a `MagicRobot` is just a special kind of `Robot`, you can invoke all the standard methods of the `Robot` class to move it around or to find out its position. To control the visibility of `MagicRobot` objects, we need some additional methods. For example, we can define methods called `makeVisible` and `makeInvisible`, which could be used as follows:

```
...
gandalf.makeVisible();      // only for magic robots
gandalf.moveTo(3, 3);       // just like a Robot
...
gandalf.makeInvisible();    // only magic robots
gandalf.moveEast();         // just like a Robot
...
```

It is also useful to be able to check whether or not a magic robot is currently visible. For this we need another method, called `isVisible`, which returns a suitable value.

What sort of value should be returned here? Clearly, there are two possible meanings to the return value – either the robot is visible or invisible. So perhaps we could return an integer where different numbers are used to indicate whether a robot is visible or invisible. This is a possible approach, but has some drawbacks. It is very common for a result or a variable to have only two possible values like this, so Java offers us a special data type known as `boolean`. Data like this has only two possible values, `true` or `false`.

The name `boolean` derives from the nineteenth-century English mathematician, George Boole, who pioneered the study of mathematical logic.

This seems to be exactly what we need. So the method `isVisible` should be defined to return a `boolean` (that is, `true` or `false`) value as shown below:

```
public boolean isVisible ()
{
    ...
}
```

To make this work, the magic robot also needs some data to allow it to 'remember' whether or not it is visible. An instance variable that holds `boolean` data is just the thing. This is defined as follows:

```
private boolean visible;  // true or false
```

So the definition for the `MagicRobot` class has three additional methods and one additional instance variable, compared to the `Robot` superclass. Here is an almost complete definition:

```
public class MagicRobot extends Robot  // incomplete
{
    private boolean visible;  // true or false

    public void makeVisible ()
    {
        visible = true;
    }

    public void makeInvisible ()
    {
        visible = false;
    }

    public boolean isVisible ()
    {
        return visible;
    }
}
```

Notice that we do not have to repeat any of the methods or the instance variables of the `Robot` class. The `extends` keyword ensures that, broadly speaking, these are available to `MagicRobot` objects automatically. There are some complexities about inheritance but to keep things simple here, we are deferring these to a later unit.

There is one slight flaw in this definition. Can you spot it? It is related to the initial state of a `MagicRobot`. We do not yet have a constructor for `MagicRobot` objects – so when we create a `MagicRobot` object, it is not obvious whether it is visible or invisible. It seems safest to make them invisible at first (so they will not show up unless you want them to). We can add a constructor as follows:

```
public MagicRobot ()
{
    makeInvisible ();
}
```

Activity 1.3
Using inheritance with a
`MagicRobot`.

In this case, the constructor for `MagicRobot` will automatically invoke the constructor for its superclass, the `Robot` class, before it does anything else. This ensures that the initial position of a `MagicRobot` object is set when it is created, just as for ordinary `Robot` objects. Sometimes the situation for constructors is more complex than this, but the details of this will be explained in a later unit.

8.3 Overriding methods

There is one further important rule about inheritance that needs to be explained. As before, we will start with a broad definition of the concept and follow this with a specific example.

When we defined inheritance above, we explained that subclasses could have additional instance variables and methods compared to those of the superclass. We also said that subclasses can modify the methods they inherit from a superclass. This modification is limited in that the body of the method can be modified, but the method signature must stay the same. This form of modification is known as **overriding** the method.

Suppose we want to define another specialized kind of robot, this time a variable-speed robot, modelled by the class `SpeedRobot`. This robot can move across the grid at different speeds depending on an internally stored step size, rather than always taking one step for basic moves, as for ordinary `Robot` objects.

So we can define a new subclass of `Robot`, with an additional instance variable to hold the step size and additional methods to allow us to set or find out the step size, or speed. The first attempt at defining the `SpeedRobot` class is as follows:

```
public class SpeedRobot extends Robot  // incomplete
{
    private int speed;  // step size for moves

    // constructor
    public SpeedRobot (int initialSpeed)
    {
        speed = initialSpeed;
    }

    public void setSpeed (int newSpeed)
    {
        speed = newSpeed;
    }

    public int getSpeed ()
    {
        return speed;
    }
    . . .
}
```

We can invoke the standard move methods, `moveNorth`, `moveWest` and so on, as the `SpeedRobot` class inherits them from the `Robot` class. However, these do not take account of the new speed data, so we need to rewrite them appropriately.

The method headers can remain unchanged, and therefore what we need is to override these methods as follows:

```
// new version, overriding previous methods
public void moveNorth ()
{
    setY (getY() + speed);
}

public void moveSouth ()
{
    setY (getY() - speed);
}

public void moveEast ()
{
    setX (getX() + speed);
}

public void moveWest ()
{
    setX (getX() - speed);
}
```

Note that the other methods of the `Robot` class, like `moveTo` and `getXPosition`, still work perfectly well for `SpeedRobot` objects and so do not need to be overridden. Only methods that correspond to different behaviour in the subclass objects need to be overridden. Here we show an example of using both the original and the new, overridden versions of these methods.

```
SpeedRobot gonzales;
gonzales = new SpeedRobot(5);   // 5 steps
Robot crawler;
crawler = new Robot(); // create normal one
...
// invoke original, then overridden method
crawler.moveNorth();      // moves one square only
gonzales.moveNorth();     // speedy robot moves 5
...
gonzales.moveTo(3, 3);    // just like a Robot
crawler.moveTo(3, 3);     // it is a Robot!
// now they are in the same place
...
crawler.moveEast();       // moves one square only
gonzales.moveEast();      // speedy robot moves 5
// now they are in different places again
...
```

SAQ 4

Given a class `SpecialRobot` that inherits from a class `Robot`, what are the ways in which `SpecialRobot` can differ from `Robot`?

ANSWER..

The class `SpecialRobot` can add functionality to that of `Robot` or modify the functionality it inherits from `Robot` or both. It can do this in the following ways:

▶ by adding instance variables to those inherited from `Robot`;
▶ by adding methods to those inherited from `Robot`;
▶ by overriding methods that it inherits from `Robot`.

8.4 Overloading methods

We complete our initial look at Java classes by explaining one further concept, method **overloading**. This is not directly related to inheritance, but it is important to understand overloading when dealing with classes in an inheritance hierarchy. First we give a definition and then we consider a specific example, which might just include a few robots ...

A class may have more than one method of the same name. However, each of these identically named methods must have a different signature; that is, it must be possible to distinguish each method from the others by the number and/or the type of its arguments. We then say that the method is overloaded: it has more than one possible implementation, depending on the arguments with which it is invoked.

So, for example, we could extend the SpeedRobot class to have alternative versions of each basic move method – one that always moves the current standard step size and the other that accepts an argument specifying the size for that step only:

```
public class VariableSpeedRobot extends SpeedRobot
{
    ...
    // define OVERLOADED method – not OVERRIDING
    public void moveNorth (int theSpeed)
    {
        setY (getY() + theSpeed);
    }
    ...
    // and for other directions, MoveEast etc.
    ...
```

This allows us to use either of these two versions of the moveNorth method applied to a suitable object:

```
VariableSpeedRobot sillyWalker;
// create a speed robot with "normal" speed 5
sillyWalker = new VariableSpeedRobot(5);
...
sillyWalker.moveNorth(); // move 5 steps
sillyWalker.moveNorth(3);   // 3 steps this time
sillyWalker.moveEast();  // move 5 steps
sillyWalker.moveEast(2); // 2 steps this time
...
```

The appropriate version of the overloaded method is selected for execution according to the pattern of arguments used when the method is invoked. This is the same approach we saw earlier for classes that have more than one constructor.

Activity 1.4
Robot world – inheritance, overriding and overloading.

Figure 16 summarizes the inheritance relationships between the classes for the various types of robots.

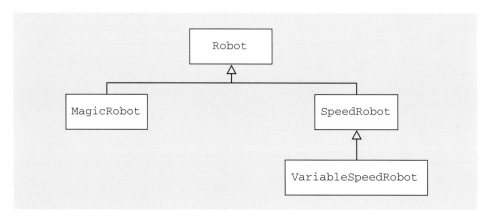

Figure 16   Inheritance hierarchy for robot classes

Figure 17 displays the positions of the robots from the different classes, after applying various method invocations.

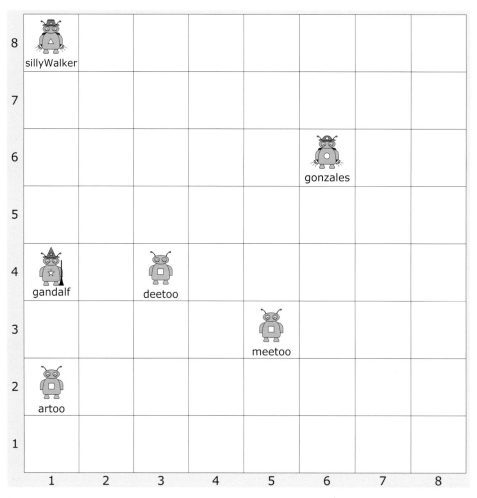

Figure 17   Grid showing the positions of objects of the various types of robots

SAQ 5

For each type of robot in Figure 16, we declare a variable and create an object of that robot type, as follows:

```
Robot r = new Robot();
MagicRobot mr = new MagicRobot();
SpeedRobot sr = new SpeedRobot(3);
VariableSpeedRobot vsr = new VariableSpeedRobot(2);
```

For each method invocation below, say whether or not it is valid. If it is, say what the effect of executing this code will be. If it is not valid, explain why.

(a) `sr.makeInvisible();`

(b) `boolean canSee = mr.isVisible();`

(c) `r.moveNorth;`

(d) `sr.moveNorth(5);`

(e) `vsr.moveEast();`

(f) `vsr.moveEast(4);`

(g) `sr.moveNorth();`

(h) `mr.makeInvisible(); mr.moveTo(5, 3);`

(i) `vsr.moveTo(4);`

ANSWERS ....

(a) Invalid. This method is defined only for `MagicRobot` objects.

(b) Valid. Stores `true` or `false` in variable `canSee` depending on whether `mr` is visible or invisible.

(c) Invalid. Need empty brackets after the method name, even though this method has no arguments.

(d) Invalid. Class `SpeedRobot` overrides this method, inherited from `Robot`, but it does not have any arguments.

(e) Valid. The `VariableSpeedRobot` class inherits this method from the `SpeedRobot` class. The robot moves to the east by 2 grid squares (which is its standard moving distance).

(f) Valid. The `VariableSpeedRobot` class defines this method as a new overloaded method. The robot moves to the east by 4 grid squares.

(g) Valid. Class `SpeedRobot` overrides this method, inherited from `Robot`. The robot moves to the north by 3 grid squares (which is its standard moving distance).

(h) Valid. The robot makes itself invisible and then moves to position $x = 5$, $y = 3$ on the grid, where it remains invisible.

(i) Invalid. The `VariableSpeedRobot` class inherits a `moveTo` method from the `Robot` class, but it requires two arguments, not one.

There are two final points about overloaded methods. First, it is not enough for two versions of an overloaded method to have different return types, if they have the same argument pattern. This is not enough of a difference to allow the compiler to infer which version to use when the method is invoked. For example, these two versions of a method called `moveNorth` would not be acceptable in the same class:

```
public int moveNorth (int theSpeed)
public void moveNorth (int theSpeed)
```

Second, the overloading may occur entirely within one class, or one or more versions of an overloaded method may be inherited from one of the superclasses. We saw an example of the latter in the `VariableSpeedRobot` class where it inherited one version of the method `moveNorth`, but also defined another overloaded version within the `VariableSpeedRobot` class itself.

9 Summary

This unit has described the origins of Java as a web technology and the aims of the language designers. Java can be used to develop both applications (stand-alone programs) and applets (code that can be included in a web page).

We have seen a number of important points when considering systems as a collection of objects.

▶ Collections of objects carry out the functions of a system by invoking each other's methods.

▶ Objects in a system can be simple or can be collections of other objects.

▶ Objects follow the principle of information hiding – their internal data is normally private and can be accessed or changed only by invoking the methods of that object.

We have introduced the important idea of inheritance, which defines a relationship between classes. This is the main mechanism for reuse in an object-oriented programming language like Java. We have also described an important graphical notation known as an inheritance hierarchy, often called a class hierarchy. This shows how classes are related to each other in terms of the methods and instance variables they inherit from each other. We have also explained the concept of overriding methods inherited from a superclass and contrasted this with overloading methods.

Much more detail about classes will be presented later in *Unit 3*. Before this, it is necessary to provide a tour of the programming facilities within Java. This is the subject of the next unit.

LEARNING OUTCOMES

When you have completed this unit, you should be able to:

▶ briefly outline the history of the Java programming language and the aims of its designers;

▶ have an appreciation of the wide range of platforms for which Java is available and the implications of this;

▶ recognize what a simple Java program looks like;

▶ distinguish between Java applications and Java applets;

▶ run a simple Java application, using the course software tool;

▶ explain the basic concepts of a system as a collection of interacting objects;

▶ understand the role of classes in object-orientation;

▶ explain how inheritance is used to design class hierarchies and to facilitate reuse of classes.

Concepts

The following concepts have been introduced in this unit:

accessor method, actual argument, applet, application, argument, assignment, block comment, bytecode, class, class hierarchy, compiler, constructor, declaration, default value, execute, formal argument, HTML, identifier, information hiding, inheritance, in-line comment, instance variable, internet, interpreter, Java, Java edition, Java version, keyword, line comment, method, method header, method invocation, mutator method, native code, object, overloading, overriding, portability, primitive data type, signature, source code, state, statement, subclass, superclass, variable.

Index

A
accessor methods 15

actual arguments 25

aims of Java language 6

applets 11

applications 11

arguments 13

assignment 18

B
`boolean` 33

bytecode 10

C
class hierarchy 32

classes 21

comments 8
   in-line comment 8
   line comment 8

compilers 9

constructors 34

D
declaration 18

default value 18

E
editions 6

`extends` 34

F
formal arguments 25

H
HTML 11

I
inheritance 31

instance variables 21

integers 18

interpreter 10

J
J2EE 7

J2ME 7

J2SE 7

Java Software Development Kit 10

K
keywords 7

M
`main` method 28

maintainability 29

methods 13
   accessor 15
   method header 7
   method invocation 13
   mutator 15

mutator methods 15

N
naming conventions 21

native code 9

`new` operator 26

O
object-orientation 12, 15

objects 12
   objects communicating 15
   state 12, 15

overloading 37, 39

overriding 35–36

P
portability 6, 9

primitive data types 18

R
`return` 24

reuse 29, 32

S
signature 25

source code 9

state 12, 15

statements 7

subclass 31

superclass 31, 35

U
Unified Modeling Language 31

V
variables 18

versions 6